When It Starts to Hurt

When It Starts to Hurt

a collection of poems

Rama Kaba

Zircon Press

WHEN IT STARTS TO HURT

Published by Zircon Press
Cover & Art Design by Alex Demanin

Library and Archives Canada Cataloguing in Publication

Kaba, Rama, author
    When it starts to hurt : a collection of poems / Rama Kaba.

Issued in print and electronic formats.
ISBN 978-0-9809432-6-9 (hardback).--ISBN 978-0-9809432-4-5 (paperback).--
ISBN 978-0-9809432-5-2 (pdf)

    I. Title.

PS8621.A264W548 2016   C811'.6   C2016-906620-7
                                                C2016-906621-5

for my daddy
RIP July 31, 2016

CONTENTS

ANOTHER KIND OF NORMAL

BONES DO NOT EXHALE

LOVE LIKE THIS

ANOTHER KIND OF NORMAL

ANOTHER KIND OF NORMAL

What do you know?
The sky is blue.
The grass is green.
In another time, another place
these could be different.

What do you know?
1 plus 1 is two
but could easily equal four.
Another mind, another calculation—
lines are never straight.
There are chinks,
but also circles with holes—
no beginning, no ending, just curves…

What do you know?
Definite articles precede nouns.
Conjunctions connect clauses.
Another writer, another story,
verbs precede nouns.
Prepositions have no sense of direction.

What do you know?
Generation cooks conventions.
Rules are meant for those stable minds
who hungrily, blindly eat it all up.

They don't want answers.
No possibilities, no imagination
except for the mould.

Objectivity is absolute anarchy.
But the norms, the traditions continue.
Those on top customize rules
even, for that other kind of normal.

CUT

The Nile slips into denial…

I'm drowning in this fissure.

Submerged in fears…

My wounds do not heal.

Forgive me—

forgive these slashes.

But these scars are mine

to slice again.

It was an unfortunate time;

I ignored the warnings.

I didn't know

I wouldn't miss.

MINDLESS JOY

Our inner-selves
accumulate doubts,
but still walk with integrity.

I'm dimwitted in open doors.
I no longer exist.
My individuality is lost
in the lackadaisical routes.

On lonely nights,
I hunger for a meaning.
Virulent whiskey is needed for the satisfactions
given and taken behind dark alleys.

Justice is no longer a neighbour.
Original Sin still howls at night.
Those damn silent yearnings of possibilities
still burn when I swallow.

How could I sate my thirst in this oblivion?

Self-awareness is a waste of free-will.

NAKED

Water gushes down my body.
I cleanse to be naked.
Bare before the shameful i
who walks, who strokes the fire.
Who dares, who tempts the night
in the light, but is too ashamed
to ever look herself in the eye.

THE TIM HORTON IN THE ROSS BUILDING

A maze of branded shoes
craft a colourful labyrinth
of rituals that have no direction.

Left tap, right cross, left cross, right tap.
Impatient feet attached to
long, short, chubby, thin legs
captured in faded jeans,
in choking cobra tights.

The tapping continues.
A band is formed
with a sigh, a moan, a groan,
and damn, a teeth sucker!

Empty pockets; TD's bright green light
beckons, and patiently waits
to refill, to perpetuate, to satisfy addicts.

Time flashes on Blackberries and iPhones.
Every few seconds, movement slips pass
the secretive time between those damn seconds.

One disappears, another appears—
this place is preoccupied
with a continuous line of conventions.

People stuffed in oversized coats;
I'm mesmerized as they undress.
Intimate habits unraveling in a public discourse:
coats, scarves, hats, gloves
disappear into pockets and backpacks.

Hair and breath wait to receive
the burning stale smell of coffee.

The chiming of abused toonies and loonies and quarters;
the throaty and rueful "Welcome to Tim Hortons"
reverberate among deaf ears
that know, that know, truly know
it isn't always fresh.

But who cares
when you're sipping
on that Timmy crack.

ONE OF THEM FEET

Michael had one of them feet.
It was big and long.
It was trimmed and cleaned.
Michael had one of them feet
that walked on bloodied soil.
That you wanted to dance on,
so you could greet his lips,
so you could place your fingertips
on his chest to feel his heart beat.
Michael had one of them feet,
that walked on hot rocks
to collect pieces of you,
so you too could walk
on roads less travelled.

WHAT I AM

There is nothing,
    nothing at all,
that can change my mind about it.

When you look,
      you look *up*.
I am that girl that sparks fire.

When you speak,
      be clear.
I only listen to what I want to hear.

The fact is truth
      is realized through reality.
Reality is what I mote it to be.

When we play,
      do not hold back.
I want those fantasies in your eyes.

I will cross that line,
      to wonder
about the how's and why's of impossibilities,

about the world's notion
of what I *ought* to be.
Which is why when it comes down to it,

I am not what I am not.
Tomorrow, I am what I was.
There is nothing in the future,

to change my mind about what I am.

WHEN I WANDER THE EARTH

I saw you holding out your hands,
like the feral Cathedral beast—
I capture your quintessence.

When I wander the earth,
I fall in love without a command.
You stole my heart near the feast.
For a minute I was of evanescence.

When I wander the earth
with you beside me, taking a stand,
how could I ever be without peace?
The angels have spoken their acquiescence.

JOURNALING

Part I

This is my story.

It's all about me.

A story all about me.

Wait.

I sound selfish but you would be too
if you had parents like mine.

You know selfish is a very funny word.

Self-fish.

Why would anybody want to be called a fish?

I am self-centered.

I am self-seeking.

I am thoughtless.

I am Inconsiderate.

Hum, I believe I'm getting the hang of this journaling…

Part II

ME

Part III

It wasn't for a selfish reason
I just wanted somebody to know
about ME

THE BEAST

The Beast:
Michael Gabriel Theodore Williamson
is a son of a bitch.
He is a father fucker,
but also a lovely mother fucker too!
He is the beast who's never cared for me.

Although this is our story,
in his version, I never exist.

I wish the beast loved me
the way he loved mother.
Was I jealous of mother?
Hell fucking yes!

How could he not see the extension
that I am?
That I am he + mother = ME

I wanted to be visible in the beast's visions.
When I needed him like all of my life,
he just looked through me.
And he was so good at it,
that I too never saw my reflection.

The Beast loved mother.
His eyes, his thoughts were all on her.

He was under her spell.

But when mother died,
I wished I still remained invisible
in the beast's eyes.

How could I have known
that sometimes it is better to not exist.

BROKEN PROMISES

I pray never to relive
the night that is extensive, soundless.

The sky is bright, yet I was abashed to look.
The stars abducted the sky.

The stars claim the sky as their own
to expose secrets in their light.

The night is meant to be dark
but provide the comfort of moonlight.

The ocean is supposed to be calm
but allow its breeze to kiss one's secrets.

However, the laws of the stars are bold.
The sun eloped with the moon.

Now, promises have no authenticity, no accountability.
The promises, you whispered in sweet tongues are broke.

Tell me how you will keep your promises
when you can no longer hide in the dark.

BETWEEN GOOD AND BAD

Fire can burn me
but also keep me warm

Water can drown me
but also quench my thirst

Food can poison me
but also feed me

Life can kill me
but also free me

Love can hate me
but also carry me

Would I know one
without the other

if I didn't have my other?

TAKE MY HAND

Come, see, touch, take my hand.

Disparity is what makes life extraordinary.
When we get together, we will demand
the freedom that should be ordinary.

Come, see, touch, take my hand.

Don't you want to escape to a better place?
Don't you know we've already trace our past
and we don't want to replace the time
between now and then.

Come, see, touch, take my hand.

Don't be afraid, we've been here before.
We've seen it before. And we've said it before.
Trust me, take my hand.
Before the thoughts of you, there was hope for you.

Let's pray.

THE OTHER SIDE

You think you know me?
Think again.
My echoes propagate through ancient walls
and break buried scandals.

I told you,
don't trust what I say—
I know desire;
I know justice.
I've seen it undulating in the puddle that is my reflection.

I speak innocence
in shattered layers.
I can utter anything
you wish to perceive.

You think you heard me?
Listen again.
I never said I was perfect;
never said I was better;
I left that for you to say.

I know the who that is me—
even under moonless, starless nights.
Even when I'm faithless, loveless
I can still seduce and excite
the other side of me.
The side that stimulates and demands attention;
the side that needs reconciliation, retribution,
but never asks for them.

Think you know me?
Think again.
There's that other side
who never comes out to play,
who perfected the art of pretending
to be everything

except for the who that is me.

THAT FEELING

Not long ago, I tried it:
popping pills like peanut M&Ms.
No separation, only desperation.
I was determined, a goal seeker—
my failures marked in permanence;
my name graved into stone.

Remember me,
remember me—
singing hush-hush.
The calm wind could not recite.

Not long ago, I felt it:
That feeling, *that feeling*,
that spins and falls between cracks,
that draws to the edge;
that keeps your hands soak
that twist your emotions raw—
a golden pear
molding and diminishing over the years.

Not long ago, I saw it:
That look, *that look*,
It looks like abandonment:
Cheese grown hard by bitterness.

A cheek still raw from your words.
The taste of anger stings
like an aged tequila from Jalisco.

That feeling,
that same old feeling,
that feeling that's old—
of waiting to be free of demons;
of wanting to cross that line.

Not long ago
I did it; I did it; I did it.
I did it to me.
Me who claims to love,
but is overshadowed by the me
who hurts so much.
Me who aches to shame, punish
into numbness—into nothingness
yet there's a tingle
submerged in that feeling.
That feeling eats me slowly
but never swallows me whole.

That feeling that enjoys never being full but fills me.

THE PAST

The music that brings tears to my eyes
echoes and vibrates among the walls of my ears.
I know I belong in the past; I'm a connoisseur of that past.
But the past would not be kind to me.
It would not be able to look past the blackness
that makes me shimmer and glow under the sun's glare.
The blackness that makes me proud of my struggles.
The colour that makes me a fighter, a survivor.
The past would not see a kindred spirit,
filled with likeness, respect, and awe.
The past would not see that I too, bleed red.

TIME DANCER

The question is not
who am I?
The question is
where am I going?

Don't be shy
to catch your reflection
to stare bashfully
into those naked blue eyes
and bear all of your lies.

You don't get to grow
without memories to show.
You don't get to love
without tears to throw.

The question is not
where are you going?
The question is
where have you been?

Don't be afraid
to recollect your past
and recast
it through the flame.

Let your energy blast through the now.

Moment to moment,
your body shakes and shudders.

Seconds to minutes,
you've sweated your own moves.

Hours to days,
you've soaked your own tune.

Weeks to months,
you've hummed your own song.

You've got reasons to belong.

Years to where you are going…
it gets better

Life is marvelous
when you dare to dance
through time.

For Jen

SNOW

You're soft and airy.
You fall quietly on the ground.

At night you shine and glow like Jewels,
like the blood diamonds in Africa.

You're never alone.
You always mingle with the earth's riches.

Too bad, so sad,
it's blood this time around.

CHILDHOOD

Childhood is meant for those who die young.
You stroke your mama's breasts awake
so she could feed your sister's worries away.
Breasts that resemble pebbles that pinch
your paper thin shoes raw.
Childhood is meant for those
whose breath smell of honey and oats,
whose sleeps are filled with dreams and hopes.

Childhood is meant for those who die young.
Every morning you caress your mama's crooked spine
straight so she could tie your brother
on her back to meet the day head-on,
You watch her tumble in the opened field
under his watchful eyes and lustful hands.
Childhood is only a dream
for those the sun has marked.

AN AGED LOVE

The despair of the golden lake

shines under the moonlight.

A lover's ecstatic melodies

forgotten over the years

are reincarnated into an aged love.

An aged love we all burn for…

USED TO

You used to tell me
when the sky turned black
and the stars wouldn't play
so I could catch fireflies
in jars, mama prepared.

You used to call me
so I could hear the residue
of your words piggybacking on the wind;
the top of my ears would burn,
and I would know your kind words.

You used to show me
what was what and what was not
cause I wasn't always on the know.
You would watch me trip
but never let me fall.

Yet, my knees are raw.

THE ONLY WAY

When you hug me
I get a whiff of dark muggy smoke
that clings on to your skin and grow cells.

Sometimes,
I would let it fill my lung,
let it coat my hair and clog my pores.

Most of the times,
it was the only way
I could have you with me.

THE SAME GIRL

I'aint that girl no more
I've got dry eyes *Restasis* can't cure.
I've got no use for tears anyways
since your actions no longer tear me up.

I don't feel that way no more
a basket of unreturned sentiments;
a limitless sky of hopes and dreams—
nah, I'aint about that life.

I'aint that same girl you knew.
Weakness no longer slips into my lexicon.
Cutting is no part of my repertoire…
Nah, I ain't about that life.

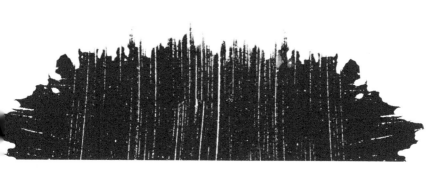

BONES DO NOT EXHALE

BULLIES

Squeeze me like a dry sponge
until I crumble like ancient toast.

Make me incomplete—
my pieces are uncollectable.

The intelligence reflecting
in my eyes remains silent—

But what is that hissing sound?

Inside this mouth,
it's a struggle
to taste, chew, swallow
sibilant phonemes.

It's a battle,
shameful,
when my tongue slips
between my teeth—

"It's abnormal,
unnatural," he says.

I get stuck;
my thoughts,
never taste my lips.

I wrap my intestine
around my lungs.

Air?

Why would I need air?
Bones do not exhale.

Their density can't bear the weight of my pain.

His laughter
still vibrates,
still crackles
what's left of my frame.

Even after all this time,
when time ceases to matter,
when there's no flesh for maggots,
it still hurts—

His words still shift my ashes.

PLAYING DEAD

I can't feel,
the sunlight,
even when it peeks
through my fingers
and chars my cheeks raw.

How could I?
I've already bared myself to her darkness.
I was a common Jezebel.
In another time, another place,
I lied for freedom.

I embrace the dark
that covers me that hides the me
who kisses the black
that marks her back
and races across her breast.

I've been told
life starts every day.
But what do I tell the ones
who die every night?
Those who prefer playing dead.

WHEN THE EARTH DIES

Where will I go?

                    North

     West   East

                    South

The four star winds are calling me.
Asking me where I want to be pushed.

Where is   Heaven

                                 Hell

How do I know that Heaven is up, and Hell underneath it.

Who came up with this notion?

Because we do not know what lies beyond the sky?
Or is it because we buried the dead?
But what about those ashes that have touched the earth's
surface?

Where will I go?

Perhaps, it is time I start following the moon that keeps
following me.
Does the moon know?
Does it know something I do not know?
Does it have something to tell me?

Where will I go?

Do not judge me.
Is there something wrong with my question?

Where will I go,
when the earth dies?

Well, perhaps the ground is better after all;
perhaps I can be that flower that grows through concrete.

HOPE

Soldiers march in lines.
Fear drum down their faces.
A bomb explodes.
Give me your hand;
I promise
I will tell your story.

THE DAY HEAVEN CRIED

I was there too.
the inked sky held your face
as you struggled to race
toward the end of your ways.

They were there too.
The angels cried.
They cried for the blood
that flows between your legs,
the blood that gives and takes life.
The life that kills other lives.

Awake.
Asleep.
Even in bliss,
life means nothing, when you have done nothing
but create the production of your own destruction.

Life has taken and collected its toll.
The lines on the road
long since faded with the never-ending
fighting, cutting, gutting, and dying.

You were there too.
But I understand why you choose to erase
the day heaven cried.

SET

Sometimes I dream
the same theme.
It's about the day
when I will dream no more.

Its many facets are still unclear,
though when I first awake it appears
as if I know the day that has been set.

But isn't that the game death plays
when the phone rings
and your father is no more.

It is here, yet it is there.
A quick turn, you might miss it.

I used to count those dreams.
But what does it matter,
when the day I will be no more
was set before I was ever more.

DEATH

Don't apologize
for the dead.

Someone has to die
so another can be birthed.

THE PUNISHER

drip

      ping,

           drip

               ping

                        down the tiles.

lifeless bodies floating on the Nile.

dancing against time,

      my heart burns for what is sinfully mine.

BARREN

I did it.   I **did** it.   I did **it**.

I ended it.   I ended it.   I end.

I like the pain.

I don't mind scorning the world for its deeds.

I don't mind making the rounds
and digging the grounds
for the seeds that won't grow.

WICKED

Birds—crows in the tree;
death is across the street.
Don't you know by sight—
witches glow at night;
druids grow by light.
Close your eyes
or you just might die.
For shame, it's wicked out here!

SILENT WHISPERS

I can hear the dead.

Lying silently on their backs.
Corpses, gently packed in dirty sacks.

Looking so damn pale,
as if murdered in a shallow dale.

Silent rivers with running streams;
a sudden scream, mayhap from a dream?

Can you hear it too?

Listen.
It's a bleep of a breath.

Do you hear the wind blowing
the leaves of the trees
whispering songs of ancient distress?

Do you hear
shadows dancing slow premonitions?

Oh listen,
don't you know by now
all things sacred are silent.

CRACK

The crack

chips away

O   so   f r e a k i n g   slow.

You bleed dry,

yet all the mistakes

you've tried to slay

still haunt your dreams.

Shit,

you're still

            b r e a k i n g.

BABY DEAD

Standing upside down—

head to toe,

eyes see a baby dead.

Can't imagine the pain.

Won't even feign

these mothering emotions.

My brain isn't trained to feel this

without being damaged.

FEAR

You taste tangy,
untraceable,
unattainable,
possible.

SACRIFICED

Since death has come to stay,
I have decided not to erase
the permanence of words
etched in anger, sadness,
frustration, disappointments.

Words written in versions
of my own truth—
are drafts that will never see their re-visions.

They are what I refuse to reveal,
to correct—the rough drafts
that rebuff rectification.

I refuse the corrected pieces
that hide the truth:

I was sacrificed to enhance his family.

TRUTH

Guilt bears no place in my mind.
When the time is right,
truth will reveal its many names.

Lies hold a place in my mouth,
because veracity ends somewhere south of—
And you can only travel so far

with authenticity as your company.

BURY ME

How do you want me?
Back flat; crack that smack I lack.

I do not exist!
But you insist!

You need me.
So how do you want me?

My words only flaunt cacophonies
of your phony lies…

Did you think I would not know your beau?
I would not blow your show?

I see your mark around her throat.
Your dark lies that float in her eyes.

That smile. That smile
that curls miles left and smirks piles right.

That smile cuts and guts me.
Buries me.

FRESH LIES

I seek what your eyes reek.

Your lies outline the shape of your body.
I am and will always be
the bloody one who knows you best.

I know the secrets you buried alive.
But you forget when you go seeking truth:
fresh lies have a funny way of reeking.

LOVE LIKE THIS

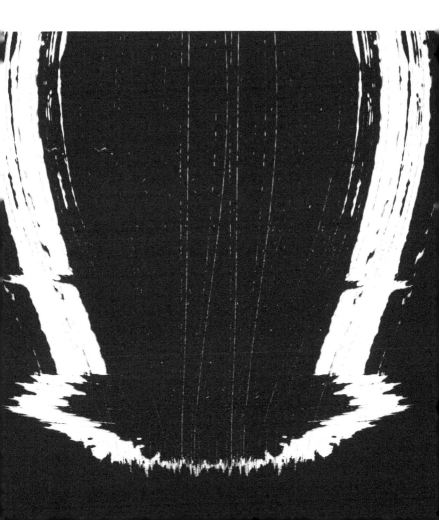

LOVE LIKE THIS

Love like this spurn Guinean gold.

Love like this makes maidens bold.

A kiss here, a touch there,
and what do you know,
I'm in love.

But, I must confess
I laugh when I'm nervous.
I laugh,
even when I hurt.

Would you be fine with a love
that is clouded by doubt and mistrust?

Because love like this,
is the only kind I have to give—

unless you propose
love unlike this.

BLOOD

You spilled
my blood.

It would be a lie,
if I loved you.

Love is a languish
I gave up many moons ago.

Love beneath that moon
lured girls with big hearts.

Zealous hands hitched to spread wide that goodness.
Fresh innocence waned with restless tides.

No sweet residue thickens the stifling air;
no screams haul on the back of the wind.

I spilled
your blood.

I would be lying,
if I said I didn't like it.

But I don't want this.
I don't want to give as I get.

INCOMPETENT

i look into you
hoping, praying
that you see beyond the masks i wear
that you hear the quiet beats my heart still plead
because every word in every language is still incompetent

YEAR AFTER YEAR

The lines under your eyes
gather wisdom so well.

I know the struggle your shoulder carries
as it arches and hunches over your pain.

I know the forgiveness your hand bears
as it trembles and rattles with grace.

I know the patience your knees parade
as they wobble and joggle with persistence.

I know the happiness your bones crack
as they stagger and shimmy with fear.

Years after years,
I know you.

I know you.
Do you know me?

MIRROR

"Mirror, mirror on the wall, who is the ugliest of them all?
You are. You are. You are," he chants.

Over and over and over, he sings.

I used to be so pretty.

"Mirror, mirror on the wall, who's the stupidest of them all?
You are. You are. You are," he shouts.

Over and over and over and over, he screams.

I used to be so smart.

Mirror, mirror, on the wall,
can you see him breathing behind me again?
can you see him touching me through the cracks?

Oh mirror,
How could this be real?
How could this be us?

Mirror, mirror on the wall,
is that blood on my reflection?

JUST A DREAM

A second,
seconds?

Or was it

A minute,
minutes?

A hand grabs me—
Neither the first nor the last:
sheets choke my legs.

This is my confession.
But this is just to begin…

I forget,

everything.   Every-thing.   Eve-ry-thing.

I forget what names you carry under your tongue.
I forget years of your filth underneath my finger nails.

I forget.

But how could I not?
Why would I not?

I was dancing in front of freedom,
or was it slumber that drugged me so?

Whose tears are those and whose bloods are these?

Was I? I was?

Why are—
I mean, who are these people?

These people who look at me.
These people who laugh at me.
These people who shake my bones.

These people who box me.

But I can't stop smiling.
I can't stop flying.

Hum, this feels strange, I'm not sure—
stop!

STOP. STOP. JUST FUCKING STOP ALREADY!

Please stop.

Why do these words reverberate among my ear walls
but fall short upon my breath?

Why is it so loud?
Stay quiet, heart.

Know this is truth.

He's coming.
He is coming.
He's almost   here.

He
never knocks.

~~He enters and I forget.~~

Leave it,
never happened.
Leave,
it never happened.

~~"Just a dream, just a dream,"~~
~~he chants in my ears.~~

"It's just a nightmare. It's just a nightmare."
I quickly add.

Hum.

INDIGESTION

YOU
heathen, weak
MAN.
I cook Plath's words.
I could chew you
for dinner and
spit you out
for breakfast.
But there's no balm
to soothe my stomach
should I ever swallow
your words.

REACH

touch me in ways
that no one ever will

see me in ways
where I have never been

please, reach into me
and take this darkness

that dwells in me

WALKED HOME

You were the one who said,
"Call me if you need a ride."
So I called.

Remember what you said?
"I just got home…."

That night,
at 10:00 PM,
I walked home.

I kicked pebbles like the way
you've walked on my heart.

Don't say what you don't mean.
Another man might be willing—

You were in bed when I got home.
You mumbled hi as I slipped in next to you.

Had you not been mine,
I would've never walked home.

GAMES

"Look here you, I'm tired. How many times do I have to tell you to never call again? That to do so, to call again would break my heart. All I want is to never fall, to never come apart. I know you don't know why I won't take a chance. But let me assure you—Forget it, I'll call you later."

DESIGNER KILLS

Hands covered in blood,
I can't hear my heart beats.
But I can hear the shadows
slowly dispending down the stairs.
They're shouting,

 "Who did this?"

A knife sticks out of my Prada;
the bottom of my Luis matches the stains
darkening my Persian carpet.

"Who did this?"

I don't remember pushing him
I don't remember my pearls snapping,
when he descended on me;
when he pulled my hair.

"But who did this?"

I can't move; I can't speak.
But I watched him fall
into the pool of his blood money.

"Who did this?"

I let money overweigh life.

ADRIFT

Madness calls me.

I trace those memories backward
so I can escape the past forward.

My thundering thoughts beckon me,
as waves lure me to my doom.

The waves are calm underneath that cold moon.
Though I love the beauty of such stillness,
I fear the silence

in our future.

POSSESSION

I can still hear him,

"Am I not all you desire?
Sweet blood drips silently.
Pain is my mine to give,
so I give it freely.

Look at me and see what lies beneath.
Ignore the trills and frills.
Let's embrace the night instead
and sing that tune our children will dance to.

It's simple really,
if I can't have you, then I shall posses you.
I take what is mine.
And if it's not, I'll simply steal it.

Inasmuch as the danger that I have inflicted on you,
I still refuse to apologize for the tears I've made you cry,
woman.
Because when you are mine, tu est à moi."

only because I need him
as a reminder that
je suis à moi.

FLY

I watch him shed his Calvin's.

We get into the tub.
The bubbles;
the soapy water
surrounds us as if we are
in Murphy's shallow pub.

Our knees bump, but I don't mind.

No, I don't mind at all.
I don't mind when he gets closer to me.
His arms warp my neck,
like an emperor capturing his Empress.

I don't mind when he kisses me.

He draws blood.
A sharp pain pierces a gap, but still I don't mind.
No, I don't mind at all.
I can now fly.

NEW YEAR

I stood and watched him, as he watched me.
We play a game of who first?
Me first, this guy caught my sight.
I sashayed with swag to present my hand.
I watched him, as he kissed my palm.
We played a game of who first?
Oh how sweet of him to have went first.
He squeezed my fingers and we danced.
The night had no limits.
We danced till the year's end.
I stood and watched him, as he watched me.
We play a game of who first.
Me first, I wanted to blow his mind.

HOW CAN YOU

How can you love me,
when I've never encountered
the part of me that deserve love?

How can you kiss me,
when my lips have never licked
and tasted honesty?

How can you touch me,
when my skin still carries traces of sin?

How can you see me,
when I've never seen myself?

STILL

All is still.
The love we once know, still.
The kiss we miss, still.
The touch, we still like.
The love, we still make sweetly.
All is still.
Especially when I look into your eyes:
I feel zilch.
Nada. Rien.

They still tell me about you.
The games you like to play, still.

You and me, we could have been explosive.
But, it's such a shame
that you still don't know my name.

FIRST

When will you come back?
You've left without a word.
Will you ever come back?

I guess your lips are still enveloped between her hips.

Your lies swallowed my lies.
I did it first, you said.
But you sure finished first.

TALK

The wind that brushes your lips
circles your mouth into a perfect O.

Warm me between these sheets
while I linger over the oohs, the aahs, the uhs.

From the sun that rises too late,
to the night that lasts too long.

Yeah, your body is mine,
mated since conception—

but can we actually talk
between the oohs, the aahs, the uhs?

WEAK AND POWERLESS

When you're old and grey...

Gather your children
for the harvest, winter is coming.
Your animals are weeping.
You can't move, you're stuck.
You're weak and powerless.

There's a grief in your heart that needs closure;
a hunger that needs to be fed.
You move with such carelessness.
You dig your long finger nails into the ground.
How soon you make your eternal bed.

Perhaps it's for the best,
since your seeds no longer grow roots.
You're weak and powerless.
But what do you expect
when you've used and abused;

when you've re-routed others' love for you.

BLAME

i can taste your disappointment
the way your eyes refuse to greet mine
the turn of your shoulder when i'm near you
the low cadence of your voice
but i wonder, if it's just your own discontent
that you can't swallow
since I've stopped
depending on you
for my happiness

SMOKE

I know you
know it was me.

I stole a pack of your cigarettes
and distributed them like twisters.

I know you
regret not calling me out.

Had you known years later that you wouldn't
be able to inhale the scent of your sweet home
would you have crumbled your cigarettes
in the sink, so that the only damage
they could have done is congested the drain?

I know
it would have been easy to fix.

Your cough wouldn't rumble mountains
and scare birds into flight.

The sight of your blood
wouldn't squeeze the small memories
I have of you.

I think you know
this memory is all
I'll have of you:

       your face masked by a cloud of smoke.

ACKNOWLEDGEMENTS

I would like to thank my wonderful husband once again for creating my wonderful book cover and inside art. This time around, I gave him complete design control and he did not disappoint!

A special thank you to Dunja for being the best editor ever! Thank you so much for taking time out of your busy hectic schedule to give me constructive feedback that leaves me feeling inspired.

In addition, I cannot express enough thanks to everyone, especially my families and friends, who inspire and support me everyday. If we've ever met or you're in my life, then you can guarantee that you will find a piece of yourself within these pages.

ABOUT THE AUTHOR

Rama Kaba grew up in the Bronx, New York City and Columbus, Georgia before settling in Ontario, Canada.

She obtained her Bachelor of Arts from York University, and her Master of Information from the University of Toronto.

If it was up to her, she would rather be reading all day instead of writing, but she does have a wild imagination that can't be contained. She also loves traveling and meeting new people.

If you would like to hear about Rama's upcoming projects, visit her at www.ramakaba.com.

You can also follow her on Twitter @ramakaba, @Chez_Rama on Instagrama and Facebook.

If you've enjoyed this book, please review and share it with others.

Thank you

For more information about Rama Kaba
visit www.ramakaba.com

For more information about Zircon Press
visit www.zirconpress.com

Zirc◆n Press